Feel your Feelings

by Scott Stoll & Sara E. Williams, PhD

Magination Press • Washington, DC • American Psychological Association

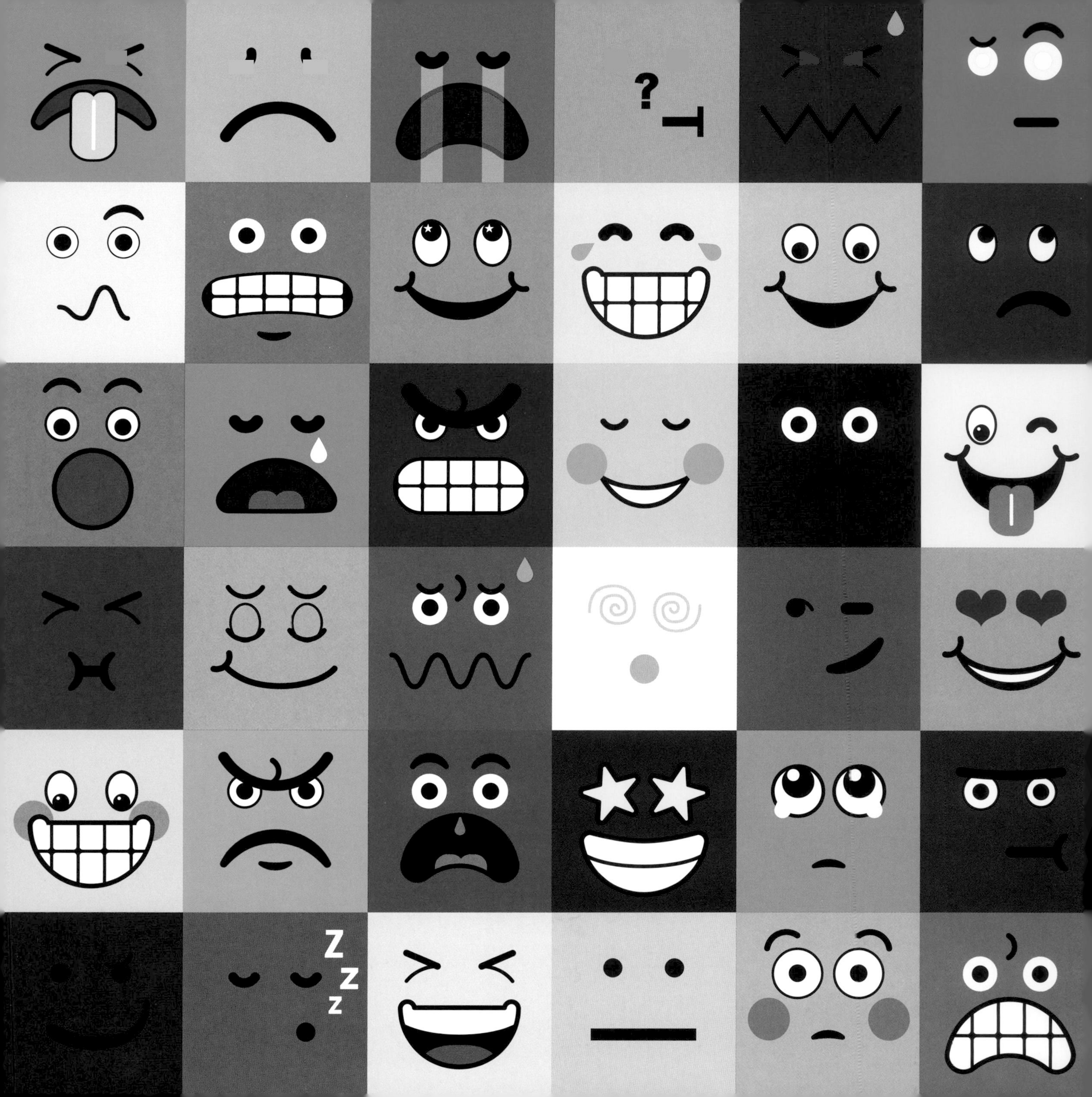

All emotions have their place.
You show them on your face.
You think about them in your mind.
You act them out all the time.

It's appealing
To feel your feelings.
We'll show you how,
And you'll be wowed!

kay, ready?
Let's feel *glad*.

Think happy thoughts.
Feel joyful inside.
Make happy feet.
Crack a smile.
Laugh out loud!

Feel the feeling!

Thank you, *glad*.
Now shake it out.
And let it go.

kay, ready?
Let's feel *sad*.

Think blue thoughts.
Feel heavy inside.
Hang your head.
Rub your eyes.
Start to cry.

Feel the feeling!

Thank you, *sad*.
Now shake it out.
And let it go.

kay, ready?
Let's feel *calm*.

Think peaceful thoughts.
Feel quiet inside.
Relax your body.
Close your eyes.
Breathe a sigh.

Feel the feeling!

Thank you, *calm*.
Now shake it out.
And let it go.

kay, ready?
Let's feel **mad**.

**Think angry thoughts.
Feel fiery inside.
Stomp your feet.
Scrunch your face.
Snarl and growl.**

Feel the feeling!

Thank you, **mad**.
Now shake it out.
And let it go.

kay, ready?
Let's feel *silly*.

Think goofy thoughts.
Feel giggly inside.
Jiggle all about.
Stick your tongue out.
Say ha HA!

Feel the feeling!

Thank you, *silly*.
Now shake it out.
And let it go.

kay, ready?
Let's feel *worry*.

Think nervous thoughts.
Feel scrambled inside.
Look all around.
Scrunch your brows.
Let out a groan.

Feel the feeling!

Thank you, *worry*.
Now shake it out.
And let it go.

kay, ready?
Let's feel *love*.

Think warm thoughts.
Feel gooey inside.
Hug yourself.
Pucker your lips.
Send a smooch.

Feel the feeling!

Thank you, *love*.
Now shake it out.
And let it go.

kay, ready?
Let's feel *disgust*.

Think yucky thoughts.
Feel sick inside.
Grab your tummy
Squish your face.
Pretend to gag.

Feel the feeling!

Thank you, *disgust*.
Now shake it out.
And let it go.

Okay, ready?
Let's feel *brave*.

Think heroic thoughts.
Feel big inside.
Puff your chest.
Focus your eyes.
Make a roar!

Feel the feeling!

Thank you, *brave*.
Now shake it out.
And let it go.

kay, ready?
Let's feel *scared*.

Think spooky thoughts.
Feel alarm bells inside.
Tremble your body.
Chatter your teeth.
Gasp in fright.

Feel the feeling!

Thank you, *scared*.
Now shake it out.
And let it go.

kay, ready?
Let's feel *grateful*.

Think pleasant thoughts.
Feel lucky inside.
Clasp your hands.
Look to the sky.
Thank the stars.

Feel the feeling!

Thank you, *grateful*.
Now shake it out.
And let it go.

kay, ready?
Now **you**.

What do you think?
What does your body do?
How does your face look?
What does your voice say?
How do you feel?

Feel *YOUR* feelings!

Now that you have reached the end,
You know every feeling is your friend.
Sad or glad, big or small,
We love them all.

Feelings paint a big picture
And make your life richer.
How appealing
To feel your feelings!

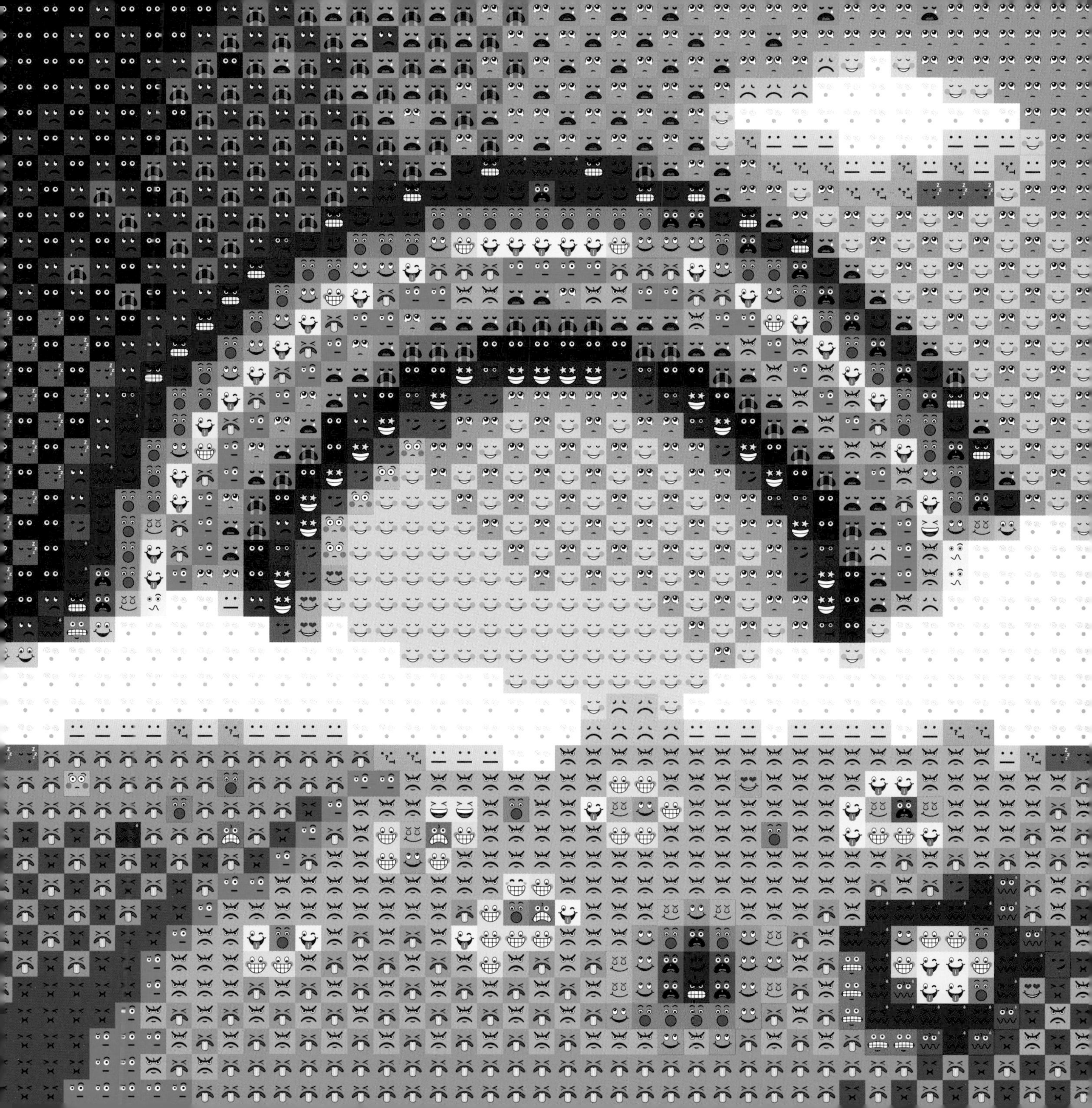

Reader's note

This is a simple book about learning how to identify and accept the emotions you have. It also creates a safe place for children to act out a variety of feelings. We say it's a simple book, but this is not something most people learn in school or at home. Having feelings is part of being a human being, but learning how to *feel* your feelings is part of being a healthy and wise human being. Teaching children to recognize and appreciate *all* of their feelings is a wonderful gift a parent, teacher, or caregiver can give. Let us explain:

The basic concept of this book

There is no such thing as a good or bad feeling. An emotion may feel bad — or as we like to say, "uncomfortable" — but that doesn't mean it is a bad emotion to have or that we should try to avoid having uncomfortable feelings. Every feeling has a purpose! As we say in our concluding poem, every feeling is your friend. Some emotions teach us what we are passionate about, and some emotions teach us dangers to avoid. Emotions are the spice of life. They are what motivate us and help form our moral compass.

Why we label emotions as bad

One reason we label emotions as bad is that, frankly, they can lead to some ugly emotional outbursts. It's as if you have a friend called "Scared" knocking on the door trying to warn you there is a fire outside. But ironically, you're too scared to open the door. So the knocking gets louder and more frantic until Scared bursts into the room and, suddenly, everyone is panicking because the room is on fire. But what if we could open the door a lot sooner and ask Scared, "What's the problem?" Scared might say, "I'm here to help. Please don't panic. There is fire, and we need to calmly exit the building and call for help."

If we never open the door to our emotions, it can lead to stress, anxiety, and even physical illness. When children understand how they are feeling and feel safe expressing themselves, it allows them to work through life's challenges and experience the accompanying rainbow of emotions.

The gift of feeling your feelings

This book isn't just about expressing emotions. It's also a book about learning how to use your emotions to create the life you want to live. It does this in two ways. First, it demonstrates that all emotions, like colors, are needed to paint a beautiful life. More importantly, it teaches children the principle in cognitive behavioral therapy that if you change how you think or you change how your body moves, you can change how you feel.

So you can see why the perfect gift you can give a child is the ability to understand, accept, and feel their feelings! And, this is a great gift for adults too. When we play-acted the book, we felt like silly kids again, yet also empowered adults. Give it a try! Your kids will love watching you play along.

About the poems

This book is written as a series of poems to help make these lessons memorable for kids and to make the book a fun read-aloud experience.

There are two types of poems in the book, but we will just discuss the feeling poems, like glad. These poems are made memorable with the use of repeating patterns and an anapestic meter that sounds like this: da da DUM.

Each poem follows two patterns. The first pattern follows the process of how an emotion is formed and expressed:

1. **Cognitive appraisal — a thought.** (Line 3.)
2. **Body sensations.** (Line 4.)
3. **Body actions and reactions.** (Line 5.)
4. **Facial expression.** (Line 6.)
5. **Vocalization.** (Line 7.)
6. **The feeling.** (Line 8.)

The second pattern teaches how to allow the waves of an emotion to come and go:

1. **Allowing the feeling.** (Lines 1-2.)
2. **Understanding the feeling.** (Lines 3-7.)
3. **Feeling the feeling.** (Line 8.)
4. **Acknowledging the feeling.** (Line 9.)
5. **And letting the feeling go.** (Lines 10-11.)

By teaching children this process, we hope that when children encounter an overwhelming emotion, they will be able to pause and think to themselves, "Thank you, mad. Now let it go. And shake it out." Then they will be better able to address the issue at hand and not get swept away by the emotion.

About the illustrations

As you can see by our cast of characters above, we chose to personify the emotions using emojis. Scott thinks they are like modern-day hieroglyphs, and while illustrating the book, Scott felt like he was inventing his own language.

About the authors

Sara E. Williams, PhD, is a clinical psychologist at Cincinnati Children's Hospital and co-director of one of the nation's leading pain rehabilitation programs. She is also a professor at the University of Cincinnati.

Scott Stoll's claim to fame is that he rode a bicycle around the world and was an honorary Cultural Ambassador for the U.S. Department of State.

Scott and Sara are also co-authors of *Dream It! A Playbook to Spark Your Awesomeness*, which teaches kids (and adults) how to use their emotions to fuel their dreams.

More resources online

Visit us online for more fun, free, and educational activities.

- Read talking points to inspire discussions about feelings.
- Download an emoji cutout kit and create new feelings.
- Learn how this book was made.
- And much more. We're always adding new content.

https://Dreamaplay.com/FYF-bonus

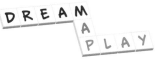

Magination Press is a registered trademark of the American Psychological Association. Order books at maginationpress.org, or call 1-800-374-2721.

Design and illustrations by Scott Stoll

Printed by Worzalla, Stevens Point, WI

Library of Congress Cataloging-in-Publication Data

Names: Stoll, Scott, author, illustrator. | Williams, Sara Elizabeth, 1976-author.

Title: Feel your feelings / by Scott Stoll & Sara E. Williams, PhD.

Description: Washington, DC : Magination Press, 2022. | Summary: "Feel Your Feelings is a book about learning to identify and accept the emotions you have, based in cognitive-behavioral principles"—Provided by publisher.

Identifiers: LCCN 2021037370 (print) | LCCN 2021037371 (ebook) | ISBN 9781433839405 (hardback) | ISBN 9781433839412 (ebook)

Subjects: LCSH: Emotions in children—Juvenile literature. | Emotions—Juvenile literature.

Classification: LCC BF723.E6 S76 2022 (print) | LCC BF723.E6 (ebook) | DDC 155.4/124--dc23

LC record available at https://lccn.loc.gov/2021037370

LC ebook record available at https://lccn.loc.gov/2021037371

Manufactured in the United States of America

10 9 8 7 6 5 4 3 2 1

Dedicated to Calvin, a cat who felt his feelings and inspired a rainbow of emotions in everyone he met.